Grasset's
Art Nouveau
Floral Ornament
CD-ROM AND BOOK

DOVER PUBLICATIONS, INC.
Mineola, New York

Planet Friendly Publishing
✓ Made in the United States
✓ Printed on Recycled Paper
Text: **10%** Cover: **10%**
Learn more: www.greenedition.org

GREEN EDITION

At Dover Publications we're committed to producing books in an earth-friendly manner and to helping our customers make greener choices.

Manufacturing books in the United States ensures compliance with strict environmental laws and eliminates the need for international freight shipping, a major contributor to global air pollution.

And printing on recycled paper helps minimize our consumption of trees, water, and fossil fuels. The text of *Grasset's Art Nouveau Floral Ornament CD-ROM and Book* was printed on paper made with 10% post-consumer waste, and the cover was printed on paper made with 10% post-consumer waste. According to Environmental Defense's Paper Calculator, by using these innovative papers instead of conventional papers, we achieved the following environmental benefits:

Trees Saved: 8 • Air Emissions Eliminated: 629 pounds
Water Saved: 2,578 gallons • Solid Waste Eliminated: 336 pounds

For more information on our environmental practices, please visit us online at www.doverpublications.com/green

Bibliographical Note

Grasset's Art Nouveau Floral Ornament CD-ROM and Book, first published by Dover Publications, Inc., in 2008, contains the images shown in the book *La plante et ses applications ornnamentales, dèuxieme sèries/sous la direction de M. Eugene Grasset* by Libraire Centrale des Beaux-Arts, Paris, c. 1898.

Dover Electronic Clip Art®

International Standard Book Number
ISBN-13: 978-0-486-99008-8
ISBN-10: 0-486-99008-7

Manufactured in the United States by Courier Corporation
99008702
www.doverpublications.com

The CD-ROM in this book contains all of the images. There is no installation necessary. Just insert the CD into your computer and call the images into your favorite software (refer to the documentation with your software for further instructions). Each image has been scanned at 300 dpi and saved in both 72-dpi Internet-ready and 300-dpi high-resolution JPEG formats.

The "Images" folder on the CD contains two different folders. All of the high-resolution JPEG files have been placed in one folder and all of the Internet-ready JPEG files can be found in the other folder. The images in each of these folders are identical. Every image has a unique file name in the following format: xxx.JPG. The first 3 digits of the file name, before the period, correspond to the number printed under the image in the book. The last 3 letters of the file name "JPG," refer to the file format. So, 001.JPG would be the first file in the JPEG folder.

Also included on the CD-ROM is Dover Design Manager, a simple graphics editing program for Windows that will allow you to view, print, crop, and rotate the images.

For technical support, contact:
    Telephone: 1 (617) 249-0245
    Fax: 1 (617) 249-0245
    Email: dover@artimaging.com
    Internet: **http://www.dovertechsupport.com**
The fastest way to receive technical support is via email or the Internet.

PUBLISHER'S NOTE

Grasset's Art Nouveau Floral Ornament CD-ROM and Book was originally published in the 1890s as *La plante et ses applications ornementales.* Its illustrations were produced under the auspices of the noted decorative artist Eugène Grasset. Grasset, born in Switzerland in 1841, studied drawing in Lausanne and then architecture in Zurich. While in his twenties, he devoted himself to painting and sculpture; after moving to Paris, he went on to design fabrics and ceramics, as well as jewelry. His decorative talents made him one of the outstanding contributors to the Art Nouveau movement. Moving on to the graphic arts, Grasset found a natural affinity for poster design, which led to commissions from American companies that appreciated his skills. He even created his own typeface, "Grasset," for use on his posters. Eugène Grasset died in Paris in 1917.

Each of the twenty-four plants or flowers included in this work, edited by Grasset, appears in a series of three plates: the first plate is a "realistic" rendering that portrays the plant as a botanical subject; the second and third plates present the plant in a highly stylized manner, suitable for textile or wallpaper design or other craft applications.

The influence of Japanese art in the use of flat areas of color and highly stylized natural plant forms (similar to those used in Japanese woodblock prints and crest designs) is apparent. Many of the illustrations in the book are the work of Maurice Pillard Verneuil, an outstanding pupil who flourished in Grasset's design workshop in Paris. As in the original work, each plant or flower is identified in English, French, and German in an accompanying caption.

The valuable contributions of Eugène Grasset's students have produced a compilation that presents natural forms in all their beauty, as well as creating remarkable illustrations that lend themselves to many modern ornamental applications. This classic work is full of surprises, revealing a nineteenth-century sensibility that is quite in step with the design needs of today's world.

LIST OF PLATES

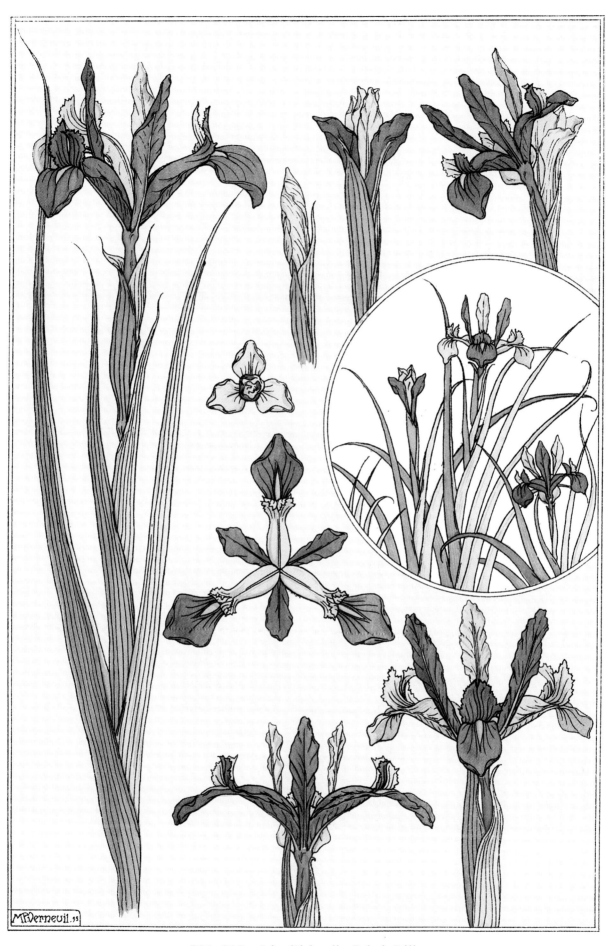

001–010   Iris; l'iris; die Scheit Lilie

1

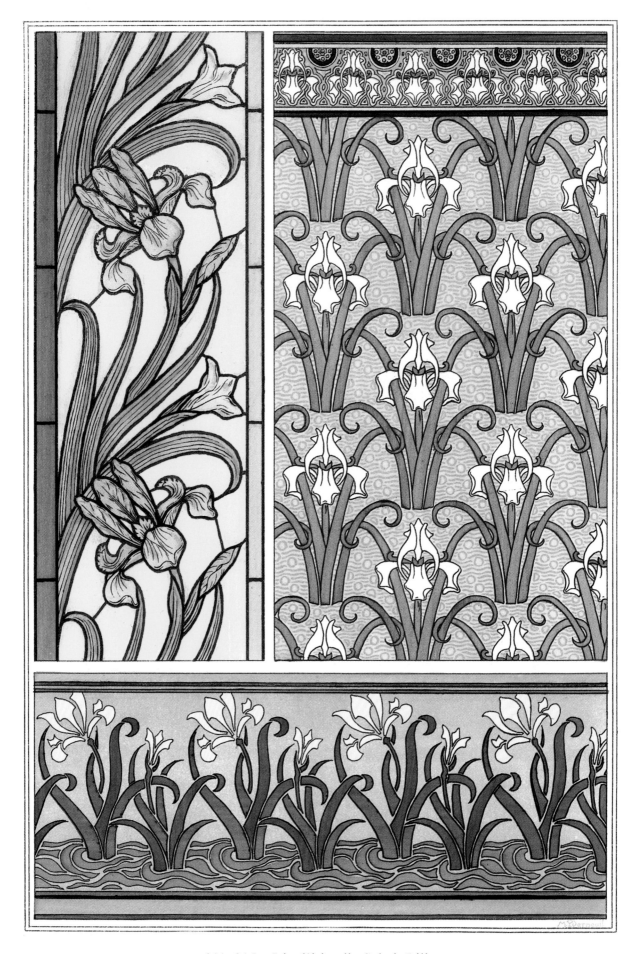

011–015   Iris; l'iris; die Scheit Lilie

016–020   Iris; l'iris; die Scheit Lilie

3

4   021–033   Poppy; le pavot; der Mohn

034–038   Poppy; le pavot; der Mohn

Marc Mangin.

039–044   Poppy; le pavot; der Mohn

045–049   Water lily; le nénuphar; die See Rose

8   050–054   Water lily; le nénuphar; die See Rose

055–059   Water lily; le nénuphar; die See Rose

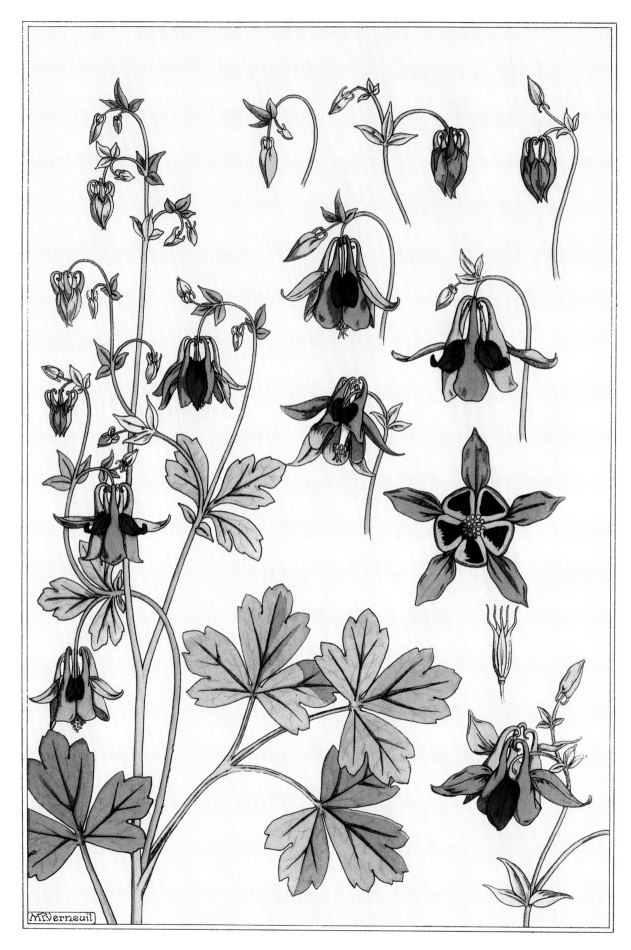

10 060–070 Columbine; l'ancolie; die Aglei

071–076   Columbine; l'ancolie; die Aglei

Anna Martin

077–080   Columbine; l'ancolie; die Aglei

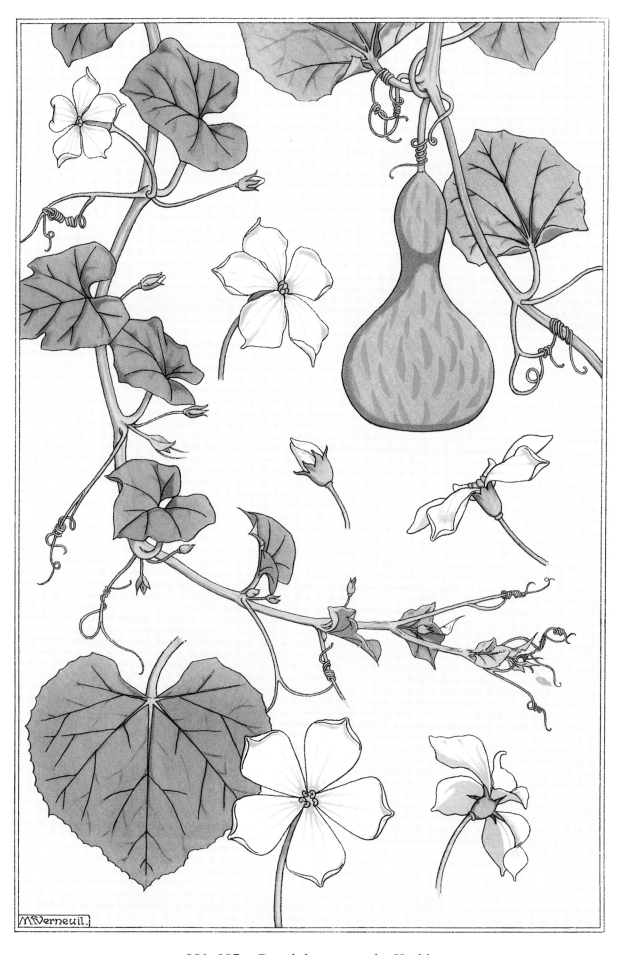

081–087 Gourd; la courge; der Kürbiss

088–092   Gourd; la courge; der Kürbiss

093–097   Gourd; la courge; der Kürbiss

15

098–105   Crown Imperial; la couronne impériale; die Nebenkrone

106–110   Crown Imperial; la couronne impériale; die Nebenkrone

17

J.Milesi

111–114   Crown Imperial; la couronne impériale; die Nebenkrone

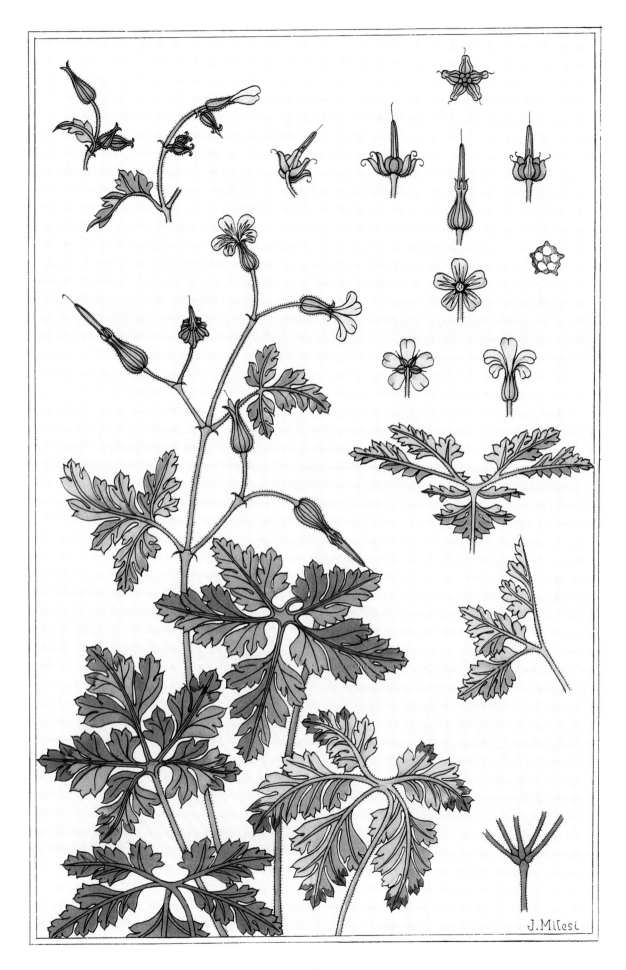

115–130   Wild Geranium; le géranium sauvage; das Geranium

19

131–135   Wild Geranium; le géranium sauvage; das Geranium

136–142   Wild Geranium; le géranium sauvage; das Geranium

21

143–155 Cyclamen; le cyclamen; das Alpenveilchen [die Erdscheibe]

156–160 Cyclamen; le cyclamen; das Alpenveilchen [die Erdscheibe]

24   161–164   Cyclamen; le cyclamen; das Alpenveilchen [die Erdscheibe]

165–170   Arrow-head; le Sagittaire; das Pfeilkraut

171–175   Arrow-head; le Sagittaire; das Pfeilkraut

176–180   Arrow-head; le Sagittaire; das Pfeilkraut

27

181–186   Daffodil; la jonquille; die Jonquille

187–191   Daffodil; la jonquille; die Jonquille

29

E. HERVEGH.

192–196   Daffodil; la jonquille; die Jonquille

197–205   Snowdrop; la perce-neige; das Schnee-Glöcken

206–210   Snowdrop; la perce-neige; das Schnee-Glöcken

211–215   Snowdrop; la perce-neige; das Schnee-Glöcken

216–224 Solomon's Seal; le sceau de Solomon; der Salomons Siegel

225–230   Solomon's Seal; le sceau de Solomon; der Salomons Siegel

231–236   Solomon's Seal; le sceau de Solomon; der Salomons Siegel

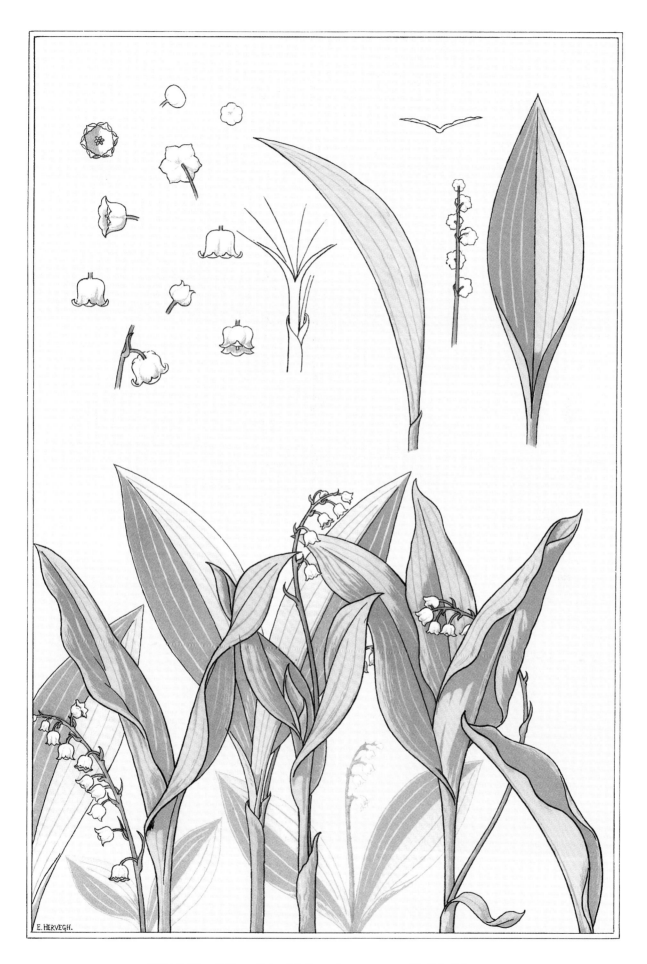

237–253   Lily of the Valley; le muguet; die Maiblume

E. HERVEGH.

254–258   Lily of the Valley; le muguet; die Maiblume

259–263   Lily of the Valley; le muguet; die Maiblume

264–271 Nasturtium; la capucine; die Kapozinerkreffe

272–276 Nasturtium; la capucine; die Kapozinerkreffe

277–281 Nasturtium; la capucine; die Kapozinerkreffe

282–291   Dandelion; le pissenlit; der Löwenzahn

43

292–297   Dandelion; le pissenlit; der Löwenzahn

298–303   Dandelion; le pissenlit; der Löwenzahn

304–310   Wisteria; la glycine; die Bohrblume

311–315   Wisteria; la glycine; die Bohrblume

316–319   Wisteria; la glycine; die Bohrblume

320–329   Lilac; le lilas; das lila

49

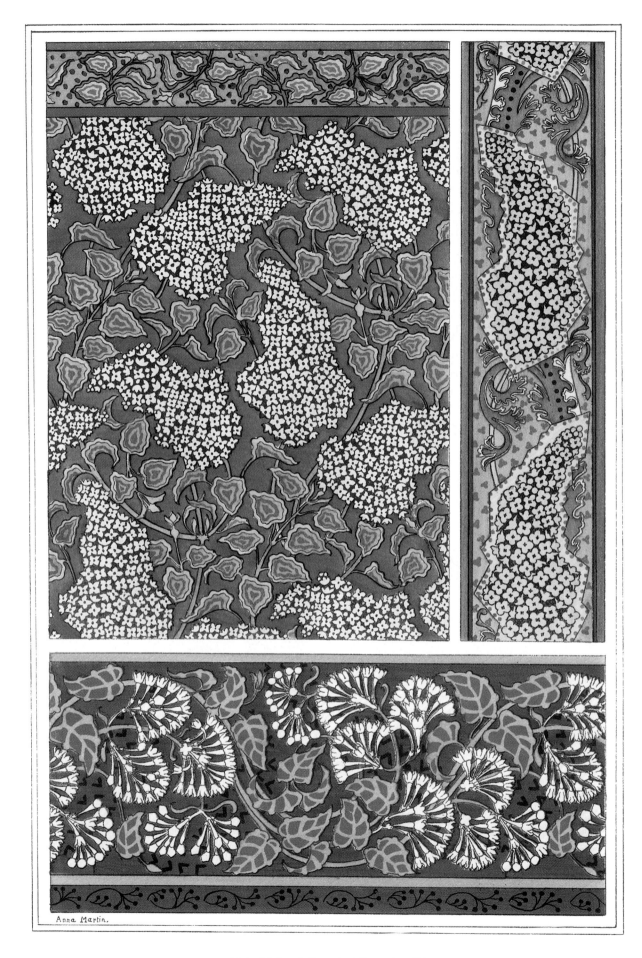

Anna Martin.

330–335 Lilac; le lilas; das lila

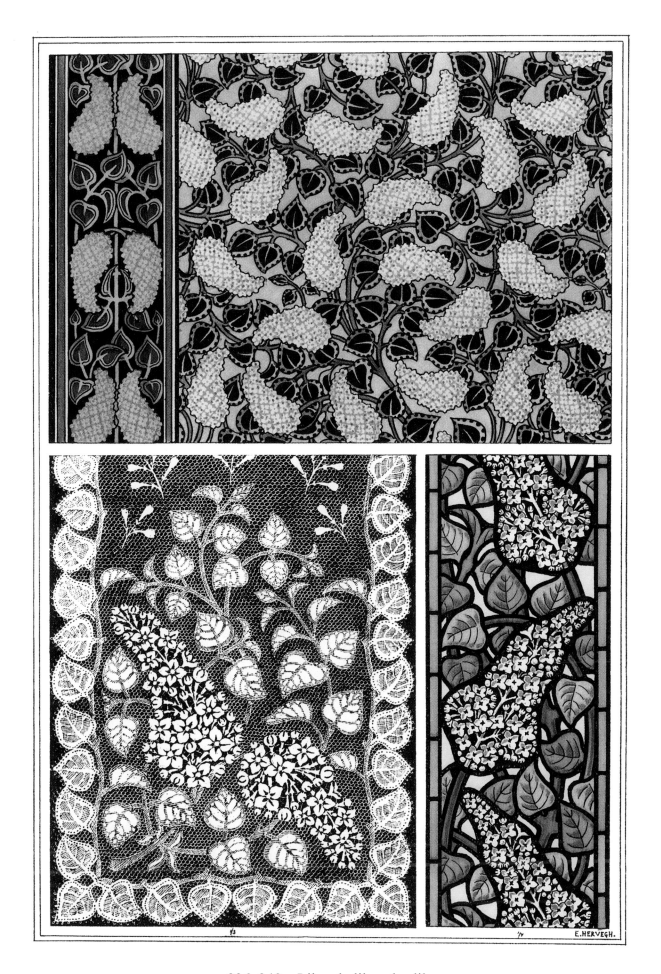

336–340   Lilac; le lilas; das lila

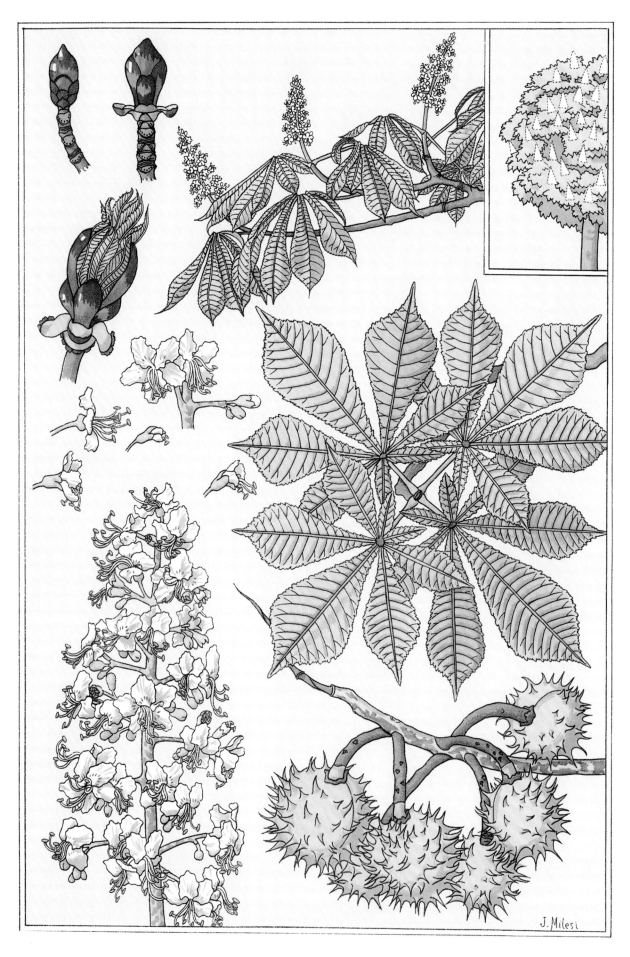

341–353   Chestnut tree; le marronnier; der Kastanienbaum

354–358   Chestnut tree; le marronnier; der Kastanienbaum

53

359–364   Chestnut tree; le marronnier; der Kastanienbaum

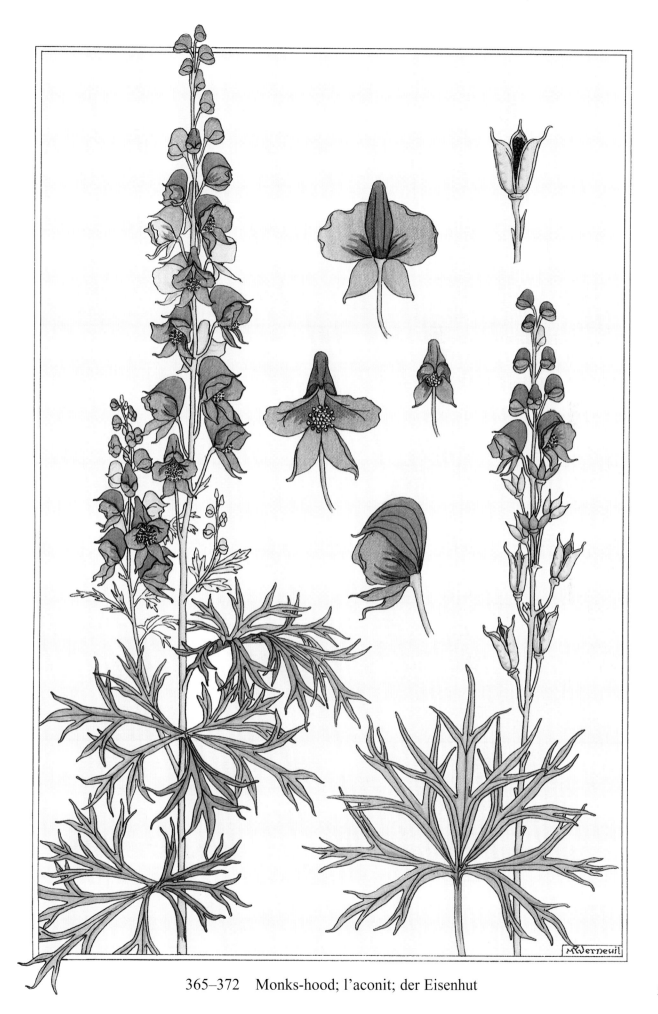

365–372 Monks-hood; l'aconit; der Eisenhut

373–377   Monks-hood; l'aconit; der Eisenhut

378–384 Monks-hood; l'aconit; der Eisenhut

385–388 Thistle; le chardon; die Distel

389–393 Thistle; le chardon; die Distel

J. Milesi

394–399   Thistle; le chardon; die Distel

400–410 Periwinkle; la pervenche; das Immergrün [das Sinngrünn] 61

Marcelle GAUDIN

411–417 Periwinkle; la pervenche; das Immergrün [das Sinngrünn]

418–423   Periwinkle; la pervenche; das Immergrün [das Sinngrünn]

424–428   Buttercup; le bouton-d'or; die Goldblume

429–433 Buttercup; le bouton-d'or; die Goldblume

65

434–438   Buttercup; le bouton-d'or; die Goldblume

439–441   Wild Rose; l'églantier; die Wilde Rose

442–446 Wild Rose; l'églantier; die Wilde Rose

447–451   Wild Rose; l'églantier; die Wilde Rose

69

70 452–455 Chrysanthemum; le chrysanthème; das Chrysanthemum

456–461   Chrysanthemum; le chrysanthème; das Chrysanthemum

462–466 Chrysanthemum; le chrysanthème; das Chrysanthemum